Now You're the Enemy

POEMS BY JAMES ALLEN HALL

The University of Arkansas Press
Fayetteville
2007

Copyright © 2008 by The University of Arkansas Press

ISBN-10: 1-55728-864-X
ISBN-13: 978-1-55728-864-6

12   11   10   09   08   5   4   3   2   1

Designed by Liz Lester

☻ The paper used in this publication meets the minimum
requirements of the American National Standard for
Permanence of Paper for Printed Library Materials
Z39.48-1984.

LIBRARY OF CONGRESS CATALOGING-IN-
PUBLICATION DATA

Hall, James Allen, 1976–
        Now you're the enemy : poems / by James Allen Hall.
            p.   cm.
        Includes bibliographical references.
        ISBN 978-1-55728-864-6 (pbk. : alk. paper)
        I. Title.
        PS3608.A54725N69   2007
        811'.6—dc22

                                        2007041678

for Dustin
&
for Brandon

Now You're the Enemy

MECHANICS-
MERCANTILE
LIBRARY.

Arthur F Mathews '06

Acknowledgments

Grateful acknowledgment is made to the editors of the following literary journals in which these poems appeared, sometimes in earlier versions:

Alaska Quarterly Review: "Naming the End"

American Letters & Commentary: "Madame Lear"

Boston Review: "Family Portrait," "Portrait of My Lover as 'Man in a Polyester Suit (1980),'" and "The Enemy" (as "Now You're the Enemy")

Diner: "My Father's Triumph" (as "The Wrong Heart")

Ellipsis: "The Dumb Body" (as "Resurrection")

Faultline: "My Mother's Love"

Flights: "Song," "In Captivity," and "My Father's Time"

Hiram Poetry Review: "Four Letters From SPC Elycia Loveis Fine"

Margie: "Safety" (as "Not Patriarchy") and "You Send Me Roses"

New Orleans Review: "Parthenogenesis"

Painted Bride Quarterly: "Portrait of My Mother as Rosemary Woodhouse," "Heritage," and "Portrait of My Mother as Lillian Virginia Mountweazel"

RHINO: "Portrait of My Mother as the Republic of Texas"

Sou'wester: "In Praise of Lies"

spork: "Portrait of My Mother as Self-Inflicting Philomena," "Portrait of My Mother as Victorine Meurent (*Street Singer*)," and "Portrait of My Mother as Victorine Meurent (*Mlle. Victorine en Costume d'Espada*)"

Third Coast: "The End of Myth" and "Pleasure"

TriQuarterly: "A Fact Which Occurred in America" and "Portrait of My Lover Singing in Traffic"

West Branch: "Wedding Dress"

The Worcester Review: "Brief History of My Mother" (as "Unknowing Her") and "Aubade"

The poems owe a debt to the time, space, and fellowships afforded by the Creative Writing Program at the University of Houston, the Writing Seminars at Bennington College, Inprint, Inc., the Bread Loaf Writers' Conference, and the Atlantic Center for the Arts. Thanks in particular to Jericho Brown, Laurie Clements Lambeth, Michael Dumanis, Elizabeth Hull, Charles Jensen, Elizabeth Knapp, Richard Siken, and Julie Wade, whose comments helped refine these poems.

I'm deeply grateful to my teachers. Special thanks are due to Mark Doty and Claudia Rankine, whose insights sparked the thinking, feeling, and writing that became the pulse of this book. I could never be done thanking them.

I am lucky to have my brother Dustin as reader, confidant, and cheering section.

Lastly, I'd like to thank my mother, Marsha L. Hall. How to say it, or precisely for what, overwhelms me. I would and wouldn't have it any other way.

Contents

I

II

I

Family Portrait

When I say my mother, the thing inside me
that strips for you begins to writhe
under burlesque lighting, leaves a sweat outline in your sheets.

When I say my father, the taunting auctioneer
comes forward and bows at the waist, smiling.
When I say my father, he hands me the camera,

he says, *Go ahead, big shot, take her picture.*
So I do, I maul her into memory.

When I say the end, no embrace, no vengeance
can bring her back. When I say I loved her,

I mean no story is true.
Not even tenderness lasts.

Wedding Dress

My mother in a white wedding dress digs a tunnel
from her father's to her first husband's house.
The dirt walls crumble around her hands, which plant,
uproot, replant themselves like bulbs in the dank earth.
The Paloma Blanca dirties, the chapel train tears.
No man, no earth could hold her forever.

Behind her, pearl and rhinestone beading glimmers
in the unfastened dark. Now in faint blue organza silk,
she digs a tunnel from her husband's house,
past the bar where he picks up his women, the lots
where he drops them off, reeling in the dew-stricken dark,

past the believing that married people do when they want
not just the story but the holes to engulf them—
she tunnels until she arrives, blushing under her veil
in my father's house. For years she stays above ground.
She lives without the dress, the digging.

But nothing can stop my mother in her Melissa Sweet,
the ruched satin too snug at the waist, her shovel ready
to injure the earth. She stands sweating in the hole,
wanting to stitch herself to the underneath,
where reinvention hides its root.

In the morning light, the man, the earth
are remade in the image of her retreat.

Portrait of My Mother as the Republic of Texas

After my mother won independence in 1836,
she dysfunctioned as her own nation, passed laws,
erected monuments to men who would never again
be slaves to order and pain.

Remember the Alamo? That was my mother.

Then in 1845 that always-pleasing church mouse voted
for annexation. My mother had too many selves and the desire
to enslave them all. Pregnant, she was forced
to become the twenty-eighth child of the American family.
Lone star no longer.

She joined a lineage of jacked-to-jesus hair, developed insatiable
cravings for honey barbecue. Her uncles sauntered up, stroked
the thin lace of her, declared she looked mighty good.
She let them say *mighty good* while grinning at one another.

Nothing grew then on the prairies of my mother.

Then she learned dissent, demanded men recognize her
sovereignty. She organized an embassy in a silver trailer
shaped like a virgin bullet. My mother renamed herself
The Republic of Texas, unfurled her flag all the way

into the 1980s, when the Republic kidnapped her neighbors,
Joe and Margaret Rowe, to highlight abuses she'd suffered.
My mother was an American terrorist.

Don't mess with Texas.

She died in the standoff. My new mother was elected
by a landslide and moved to Cuero, a city whose largesse
depends on retirement pensions. My peaceful mother
holds weekly rallies: "What do we want? When do we want it?"
Her lipstick stains the bullhorn mauve.

In her spare time, my mother receives foreign dignitaries
and does drywall. The Global Conglomerate of my Mother
opened her first staffed consulate in Barcelona.
She insists visitors speak American.

Currently, the Republic is facing lean times.
The former treasurer neglected May's utilities,
refuses to return the funds. Pledge your support today.
My motherland is standing by
the rotary phone, waiting for your call.

Love her or leave her.

The Egg

It's the last egg in the whole world.
The world is a single-wide trailer,

a three-year-old at his highchair.
The child slams his fists

on the plastic tray table, screaming
at the top of new lungs, *I Want My Pancakes.*

The child wants so much
from this tiny world.

The pregnant mother spent the morning
with her head at the toilet, in the cramped heat

of the trailer. She has not asked to be
this world's small god. *I Want,*

the boy begins, and before she can
stop herself, the god screams back,

Here's Your Goddamn Pancakes! The egg
hits the child on the forehead and breaks.

The world is quiet. The egg slides down
the child's face, a trail of shell and yolk

and the child's tears. The god feels rage
and pity. She calls her husband home;

he wipes the dried egg from the adopted
son's face, then soothes his wife, holding her

to his chest in their bed. When his wife
and son are both sleeping, the father

cleans the broken egg with a wet washcloth.
The world gleams again.

The father sits in a chair in the kitchen.
He takes measured breaths, he wants

to believe the world will be different for the next one,
the one he does not want to be born.

Portrait of My Mother as Rosemary Woodhouse

My mother dreams she's adrift on the Adriatic Sea,
naked elderly men and women lounging all around her.
Blue waves slap against her thigh, and stones fall
from unspeakable cliffs. I am dropped
into her, boulder after boulder of me,
until I am safely drowned inside her.

                        In the morning, Manhattan
never looked so peaceful. "I dreamed someone
was raping me," she says, shaking her honey-blonde hair.
"Thanks," her husband jokes, displaying newly manicured nails.
"It was kind of fun, in a necrophile sort of way."

My mother marks my due date on her kitchen calendar.
The red circles stare back matter-of-factly.
These are horrible times.

A month later, my mother accuses Dr. Sapirstein
of poisoning me. My mother fears her life has ended,
her life has grown beyond her, her life will sprout
a hybrid black bloom. She packs her one bag,

runs from her husband's house to the refuge of Dr. Hill,
her first physician. All around her, women slow to a blue wintry blur.
A flurry of women lay their hands on her stomach
chanting, "Pain is a sign something awful's happening."

My mother does not heed this loose-tongued omen.
She stops in at Vidal Sassoon, steps out reborn:

the first modern woman, her jaw line fixed parallel
to the city's trash-strewn streets. She envisions such elegant escape.

Dr. Hill's surprised to see his former patient. Imbued
with the power to overlook narrative gaps, he does not flinch
at her story. He's the promise of good in a darkening nation.
My mother prays God will bless Dr. Hill.

But the story of belief runs parallel to the story of betrayal;
my drugged mother gives birth to a living death.

After weeks of hearing my crying, my mother dismantles
the false wall with the plastic crucifix, she explores
the passage from the dream world to the one
whose reign I herald, the world of hoarded women.
Entering with a knife, she emits a battle cry
and spits in her husband's face. Her wrath slides down
his cheek. When I begin to cry again,
she wants to hold me, she drops the knife.

The dream of the knife becomes the story
of a generation full of black bassinets. In the story,
all along, the naked bodies were real.
Covens are a fact of America.

And I am the thing most coveted, the proof
my mother loved each of her ruinous children well.

Song

Then I was shattering, not just broken,
but the force behind the breaking—exquisite,
a low, unstoppable voice.

The nurse pushed on my mother's stomach,
her fingers curled underneath her palms.
My mother's rapid heart told me, *Be afraid.*

In the sober white room, my mother said, *I'm warning you.*
The nurse didn't stop: it was her job to separate us.
My mother's fist drew back. My father caught his wife's hand

too late. The nurse stumbled backward, breaking
a tray of sterile instruments, her bottom lip bleeding.
The doctor, crouched between my mother's legs,

could not tell which woman he found more beautiful:
the one falling back in fear, or the one whose fear
was filling the room with sound. My mother's hand,

the nurse's mouth: I was born between them, calling
from the open wound, wanting to heal her
even before I could be heard.

Touch

She won't turn her head, won't lift her arms.
Her stare doubles the distance
from which we call, my brother and I.

In her bed, her body shakes, trying to render
imperceptible the panic she feels.
The years she froze her body

no one can break into now. She whispers
the word "hands" so fast it becomes brittle,
sounds like "Shands," a hospital in Gainesville, Florida,

where the doctors cut my two-year-old body.
But she's not in that emergency room,
she's flooded by the red touch of the past.

My mother wakes because she can't breathe.
Her father's beard burns along her bottom lip.

His mouth opens her mouth.
Then her legs, his hands between them.

Her body so thin the kids in her class
call her zipper—now the zipper

ungathers in the dark, cleaving its own kind.
Now his body pushes down into the mattress.

Tiny gray hairs across his chest flutter.
Now she's on hands and knees, escaping

out the open window of the mind
until she is safe in her sister's bed,

where another girl waits to be next.

After, the father reads from the family Bible,
the sisters sweat out the hushed tones
of Genesis until he is tired, convinced
his sleeping girls love him. The girls shudder

in their dreams, clawing at each other's faces,
unwaking through the hours of the last night
he'll touch them, the night they begin to bleed.

A Fact Which Occurred in America

In the fifth grade, when we came finally to the Civil
War, the teacher kept saying, *We lost, we lost,*
his eyes a shadowy grief under his favorite painting,

a laminated Dawe reproduction subtitled *A fact
which occurred in America:* a black man wrestling a buffalo
to the ground. The ground becomes his grave, I am the buffalo.

In the painting of the buffalo rolling his eye
to size up the man who will never be strong enough
to wrestle his way out of the definition of black,

I am trying to say, *We are metaphors for each other, please
don't kill me.* The man is black but so is the buffalo,
so is the sky and so is the heart which keeps this fact holy.

In the painting I am the buffalo because I want to be loved
by pure physicality, a man with broad hips and broader anger
and a yoke around his neck which has not broken him

yet. In the painting about a buffalo's last breath,
I am the dust matted on the lips. Kiss me, keep me
in your mouth, don't let me dissolve into fact.

In the painting about a boy who writes, *I am sorry we lost
the Civil War* fifty times on the blackboard after school
in his deserted fifth grade class, I am the bone-white chalk,

I have always wanted to be someone's defiled good buffalo.
In the painting the man tells the buffalo, *Play dead,*
I'll get you out of this. In the defiled fifth-grade teacher's

laminated copy of the painting, I am the racing pulse
of the boy getting his revenge when the teacher isn't looking.
I am the time after we learned about the heroic Civil War,

on the playground when Day-Trion caught me alone
in the maze of trees and held me down with one hand,
kissed me with his tongue, licking my lip first, smoothing it

for his, my first kiss, on the ground, the leaves spreading
under us, black and wet. Deep in the animal-wrestled-down
part of me, the boy was bent like a tree over a maze

scribbling a hyphenated name in tiny scrawl in black ink
on a piece of paper, trying all hour during language arts
to get back to the maze when the teacher snatches up the paper,

his eyes widening at the darker revolt.
In the punishment, I was the blackboard, my body
lashed by loss and sorrow. I was the buffalo,

I wanted to lose the war; I wanted to stay black,
the filmy white chalk a sickness stretched over my skin.
In that America, I am always betraying the master.

Family Portrait

If I could turn the photograph, bring my mother's face
to the bright eye of myth, my unflinching lens,
you'd see she's mouthing the words: *Take the picture already.*

You'd see my father's lust, his loathing
molding her body into some four-legged
photogenic thing, whipped and adored.

You'd see my mother emerging from the ghost world
limb by limb, carrying on her bowed shoulders
Eros and his sadomasochistic twin.

In the dim violated light, she's marked
by a man who can't let any part of her go.
In the light my father makes in the dark,
I was mothered into art.

Portrait of My Mother as Self-Inflicting Philomena

The man on top of my mother waits for her
to turn into a winged, calling thing.

Now that he's captured her, he's thrilling
in her throat, flattening it with his hands.

The woman under him is guilty, mutable; he gets to judge
what she will become. The tongue, the tongue—

he knows she'll use it when his grip loosens.
His grip rules her out of wren and raven

and pigeon and lark, blackening out the hours
of the avian July sky. The man knows how

to press a woman's face into the hardwood floor,
to wear away her nose skin, make the foul bones show.

He knows the body can become its own enemy.
The man and my mother have been lovers;

they've tried on each other's skin,
dressing in the other's clothes, going out renamed.

They stumbled home, those nights, tearing away
their clothes, their taped bodies scraped raw.

And that's what it takes, memory of her skin,
to make him roll off of her. He can't face the animal

he's become. He walks, calm, into the kitchen.
Calm, reaching for the gun.

≈

My mother runs even before she's upright,
out the unlocked door, down the concrete stoop,

pulling up her pants, over the lawn,
into the Sunday traffic, waving her hands,

saying *Help* in a voice she does not recognize.
In the street, man after man slows but does not stop.

Behind her, her lover opens the door, the shotgun still in hand.
Come back, Marsha Lynn, don't you make this worse.

But a car of women stops, my mother is rescued.
Later, it looks like grace, his decision

to let her go; it helps her believe he's sorry,
it will never happen again.

Days later, she's climbing on top of him
in the cot, believing him when he says

she is beautiful, hoping this will heal her. The man moves
quietly underneath, handless, a meek thing—

except when he's calling her name
in a voice indistinguishable from her own.

In Captivity

She was just one of a cavalcade of kneeling brides,
women wiping the mouth clean of color
before throwing themselves out of bed at midnight,
stealing the horse, galloping away into the breathy husk of night,
her ears filling with the sound of the master
in close pursuit. She was one of these women
who awaken after the fact, overlooking their lives
at the edge, who try to fill the lungs with air
enough to float down the cliff and into the sea,
the man behind her dismounting, laughing.

The question is not, was my father one of these men,
was he possessed by her, was he a horseless victim.

Was he patient, did he wait until they were home,
in the rumpled marriage bed, to teach his wife a lesson.

Was he laughing when the sobs filled like saltwater in his wounded body.

The question is, why—after he stripped the mare
of her bridle and bit, there at the cliff—why

did my father wipe his pistol clean
before he shot his favorite horse?

Safety

The father does not knock on the locked door *
gently, as if loving a small hurt thing.

The father does not say *Please* over and over,
until his voice becomes unraw with the not-said.

The mother inside the room
does not hold a gun to her chest.

The mother did not make the father
into what stands knocking: a safety

the mother clicks on and off.
She has not just ended an affair

with a brutal, brutal man.
The mother's heart is not broken.

The children are not asleep in their rooms.
They will never know how close

the mother comes to the trigger,
they will not grow up

to take the father's place.
The father is the mask, the terrible delay.

My Father's Triumph

In her amber nightgown, waiting by the front door,
my mother is sheer goddess, marred only by morning hair.

My suited father ties his hands around her,
leans forward as she leans backward.

Her hand flutters to his chest.
My mother opens her eyes, she says *I lush you.*

Every morning, this mangled phrase leaves her mouth.
Harm done to the word is done in the chest.

My mother shuts the door. I am called to her
by her sighing, the car's wheels turning onto the road.

I belong now to my mother, who has just returned
from some other house where a man did not worship her.

My father could not bring her back for so long.
The night he triumphed, I saw him naked

through a crack in their door. I began
examining myself with a flashlight under the covers.

I am his body. I will become a man
and will not know how to be radiant.

My mother, my father: only one of them
can be saved, and my heart is the wrong heart.

Parthenogenesis

Every year we watch a man crown some rubicund not-me
or my mother Miss USA. *Mom, why don't you enter?*
You're prettier. We study the contestants, betting on the winner.

My favorite, Miss New Jersey, advocates her charity:
Nancy Reagan's "Say YES to Drugs!" Her face never loses
its luster, even when tuxedoed arms muscle her off to some dark cave.

I envy this loser's wide sash of mouth, though I'd never admit it to Mother,
who knows terrible names for things: *silicone implants, judge tampering.*
She is the most beautiful woman in the world.

While we watch, I'm reading an anemic version of *The Iliad,*
which wizened Athena, posing as silver-bunned librarian, prophesied
fourth-grade me wouldn't have a chance in Hades of comprehending.

I'm enamored of plotting goddesses and trophy wives. On commercial break,
I twirl my mother's Pall Mall Menthols between my lips,
imagine myself Helen of Troy, the tiara-toting Empress of Deportees.

I want to be irretrievable among men and gods. The librarian
is right. I can't master Paris's *amour* for Helen, she of ambiguous passions,
ivory-glinting arms. What addicts me to beauty is Cassandra, enslaved

by her own words. Omen-eyed, she vetoes the god's advances,
presides over the parade of Patroclus and Achilles and Hector,
their loinclothed thighs charioteering toward me.

But worshipping other beauties provokes my mother.
She demands I abjure my idols, become her
sole devotee. And so I am allied to the queen—

an unbelievable boy, divining the city of her ruin.

My Mother's Love

My mother feeds the multitudes of abandoned cats
that live in the field behind our office. Every sundown
she untangles fur, feline lineages. She names each one.
And though they are legion, she does not forget.
She administers heartworm medicine to one hundred
feral cats. She cradles them. Imagine her
frenzy, then, the day the bulldozers come,
a sudden god-congress in the air.
The cats hunker in their homes in the ground.
The bulldozers begin their awful roll. My mother,
at field's edge, waves her arms, a decoy.
She stands in front of the men and their stomachs,
big rollers of flesh. She does not move, she shouts
until their faces dampen with her spit. She hears the earth
fill with mewling. She digs, she saves thirty-two cats that day,
then takes them home, bathes them, speaks to them calmly
even as they claw up and down her arms. I'm her
witness, I'm buried in this story, down in the place
where collapse is inevitable, where love is
only love if it makes you bleed.

Family Portrait

The woman has disrobed, bent forward, turned her face
away, knelt down until her elbows indent the floral bedspread,
spreading her ass for the camera.

The woman is a bottle blonde with limp hair, parted exactly.
A thin line of pink scalp divides her in two:

woman brave enough to transform herself
into glinting-armed, bowed-shouldered, Polaroid porno model

and the mother who turns her face so she'll see
only the shadow self taken prisoner.

The next day, my mother left my father.

Madame Lear

I never exited stage right.

I never abandoned Kent, his open-eyed jealousy,
his tendency to hide inside our closet.
I never left him alone with my gowns.

I never left Regan, her diatribes against the country
I fostered into ascendancy.

I never deserted Goneril; her open-jawed guffaw
never haunted me down the halls, out into the garden,
down cliffs, into the roiling waves, all the way to France.

All my children sleep like sharks, eyes wide
through the streaming rush of plot.
My daughters never preyed upon me.

I never left them in my heart.

Howling nights, I lay with the fool and asked him
how one leaves a self. The fool's answer
fouled my mind forever.

I never left Cordelia, her inability to mend
her tongue, her father's injured speech.

I never stepped outside the drafty palace. I stayed
curled up in the bushes at night, I perfumed the air.
The leaves scratched my eyes out.
I never looked back.

When I never left, a fire was dying in my room.
I never let my children in there
to warm their hands at my absence.

Brief History of My Mother

My mother, fourteen, makes a girl
eat an entire can of Alpo.

At forty, she leaves her husband
for a man who wears women's underwear.

Every Friday night of my childhood, she's criminal.
The door creaks open for the same cop, his broad smile.

Bank of America calls for Marsha Hall.
I'm not in right now, she says.

My mother, thirteen, smokes mentholated cigarettes.
The burn dissolves to a tight hiss on her thigh.

She wakes to her father's kiss and cannot breathe.
My mother promises, *The abuse will stop with me.*

She tries to die, once, by swallowing pills, choking
them up as I hold back her hair.

In green pants, orange sash: Miss Safety-Guard,
1982. She blacks out her front teeth, smiles at men

who cat-call to her on the corner, her stop sign in hand.
Their faces quicken from the slap of her unbeauty.

Tries to die, once, by standing in traffic
on a dirt road at 3 a.m. My mother, desperate for a Mack truck.

My mother asks the doctors to turn off her dying
father's respirator. She watches him struggle to breathe.

My mother's tombstone will read,
Gone to see my mother.

II

"*Divorce me, untie, or break that knot again,*
Take me to you, imprison me, for I
Except that you enthrall me, never shall be free. . . ."

—John Donne

Pleasure

I chased my older brother into an orange grove,
calling his name. He sat in a tree, becoming a hard
thick branch I could never reach.

He and his beautiful friend laughed, threw oranges
that splintered into scent on my knees, the back of my head.

I wanted to turn into something so beautiful
the oranges would stop. Or I wanted to become a hole
that could catch and save them.
My body, the death of oranges.

When I fell down, the fruit burst over my thighs,
the small of my back. There's no hole on earth
where the heart drops through
without bringing something with it.

The earth did not grow under me.
I pressed my mouth down into dirt.
A kneecap of an orange shoved my legs apart.

The brother who turned into a tree, the terrible friend
who threw moldy oranges until another body submitted
to pleasure—each taught the prostrate supplicant
how best to worship the men who would be gods.

Heritage

1.

One night, when I was seven, I fell out of the top bunk
without waking. A dream absorbed the pain.

When I woke, it was still dark out, the middle of some night.
I walked down the hall to my parents' bedroom.

I could hear them awake. My father was beating my mother.
His slap was quicker on her flesh. I wanted to break

the door down to stop him from hurting her. Then my face
turned red. The word *sex* blared loud

as when Tony Camacho said it in class
and Mrs. Morrow spanked him bare-assed in front of us.

I went back to bed. It remained dark outside
for several hours. The sun rose, another slap.

2.

The men in the photographs never have heads.
They are giant cocks, shaved balls.

I want them to have eyes and lips.
Their words would make me whole.

My favorite: nameless jock in white plastic shoulder pads,
the eye-black grease glistening in the lights. Even his dick is tan.

The cheerleader's head tilts toward that bronzed find.
Her tongue juts out. Spittle gleams along her bottom lip.

She is a pair of legs, splayed on the locker room bench,
all misted flank and shaved crotch.

This is the gods' fiery postgame hunger, the devouring
I welcome with my opened mouth,

my sawed and truncated wanting.

3.

My best friend likes to model his boxer briefs,
to walk in on me urinating. My best friend lies

on his bed, hands thrown up over his forehead,
chest bare in the moonlight, his body not pornographic.

Pornography is a fantasy made with real bodies,
lighting them in dark rooms so the skin glows

almost blue, airbrushing away any devastation.
I try hard not to see my best friend in his underwear,

not to imagine him on top of me, moaning.
Pornography is a vow to try harder: reverence

these others, the film says, covet only what's untouchable.
I swear to God I am not thinking of his tongue,

the pink rawness of him, I swear to God I am not in love
with my best friend or his hairy older brother.

I am a fantasy he fashions, his legs spread. To speak
would shatter the fantasy. I know my quiet place.

I know to stop when his hips slow their spasms.
Nothing is more real than licking your best friend's asshole.

Afterwards, we sleep on the floor, the bed between us,
a borderline he calls the *fag divide*. We dream our separate dreams.

4.

My mother shows me the magazines she's found
under my mattress. The men and women posing
in and then out of uniform—they'll never be true.

I name the man in the picture Sean.
He moans when I swallow.

My mother makes me cut the pictures into shreds.
She points to a naked woman holding a leash.
My mother says I believe women are dogs.

I've been erect in front of that picture, begging
her to leap out of its frame, this flawless redhead
brushing her smooth legs up and down my thigh,
licking my earlobe and saying my small name.

The leash is limp in her hands.
Something in me pleads
to be chained in her bright shame.

We Fall in Love with Total Strangers

We were stopped in her car in the parking lot
at Winn-Dixie. It had begun to rain,
the wipers wouldn't work. The red neon sign
failed to illuminate the darkness the storm brought.
My mother turned to me and said, "Will you forgive me?"

We hadn't been talking before the storm. I was barely fifteen;
I didn't even know how to blame her yet. She said it again,
her voice hoarse and religious in the overdramatic rain.

Just one week before, I'd been kissed by a man. In an empty
hospital bathroom he pressed me against the sink,
my back bending toward the mirror. The light seemed to gasp.
The man—a nurse?—flattened his hand against my zipper,
lowered it until I emptied out. And then the kiss, like steel
softening in wettest dark. I kept my eyes open.

When he stopped, I told him I loved him. He was bending
to kiss me, I was closing my eyes when he lurched back.
His hand became a memory on my ass. Whatever throbbed
in him flickered. He saw me for what I was: a flood of need.
I said, "I didn't mean that." But will you forgive me
is an incurable question.

The rain stopped. In the wet stillness I slid my hand
to my mother's. It was cold and she was crying,

the man had hurried out on her too. In the well of my throat,
everything I wanted to say was dangerous.

She was cold. The words a boy says to comfort
his mother swam closer. I drew them slowly
out of me. I left the rest to drown.

In Praise of Lies

The woman who taught me to curse first gave me She-Ra dolls.
My favorite, flame-haired Cast-a-Spella, crumbled castle walls
with the furious blue heat of her incantations.

                And so I learned early
the world changes to better deserve the princess warrior.

My mother told me I had a beautiful face.

Later, when a boy at school called me "faggot," my mother overheard.
She flashed her badge, threatened jail time. She was a crossing guard,
an abuse of power in steel-toe boots. My mother taught me
"may-el-ven-ee," Finnish for "go to hell."

                For years, I fouled my enemies
with gibberish, believing her words protected me.

The day I came out, we argued in a kitchen. Our fight heated
beyond repair. She charged, her fist a glimmering horde of steak knives.

I struck my mother down and my father took her place.
I struck my father down and I took his place.
Something cobbled from the wreck rose in my stead.

It did not have a beautiful face.

                Wherever my mother is tonight,
praise her. She invented the woman who taught me passion,
not beauty, is the mother of truth.

Bad copy that I am, I can only turn to ash She-Ra's plastic fortress,
every cave that shelters the monster who serves my mother still.

Portrait of My Lover as "Man in a Polyester Suit (1980)"

This is how I've changed my life: I've fallen in love
with the Archaic Torso, clothed him in modern garb

made from sheer synthetic fibers, the torso obscured
and buttoned up, fettered and lean, framed

in a reserved three-piece ensemble, shining in the light.
This is how I'll worship you: from your knees

to your narrow chest—you exist only in parameters,
and you only exist for me. I want you, cut

this way and pieced in the light. And loving and light
are brothers, two smooth blades fastened into shears,

trimming and trimming the body. I've dressed you
in a rumpled suit; it's been worn, funerals and weddings.

Your hands by your side, your zipper undone. Looking
at you is my fetish, a grafting of the mind's stain

onto the muslin canvas of the flesh. This is how you live forever.
In my mind, the unrested part of me. My solitary days

and sullied nights, you held me down so I could not see
your face, you growled obscenities until I writhed,

and then you quieted, you left your musk and lavender,
you were as if I'd never breathed.

This is what the camera doesn't capture: your arched neck,
the long throat curving backward, out of view, a contrast

to the gentle arc of your cock. I can't show anyone
the curve of your mouth, how you'd say my name in flashes,

piecemeal, like the Orphic penitents always do, before
they close their eyes and push the body down the river.

Portrait of My Mother as Lillian Virginia Mountweazel

Most of all, my mother wanted to mean something.

The desire consumed her—like it did Lillian Mountweazel,
who devoted her life first to photography, then weaponry;
she too wanted to go on transforming the flesh
from the real into the tortured. My mother

was filled with wanderlust, a legion of mercenaries
setting their campfires on the beachhead, scoring fear
into the adversary, watching from the walls.

Most of all, she wanted to tongue-lash, to conquer
the barbaric fathers, then govern their bodies.
Incurable among the battle lusts, she lay down
her camera to fight. In this photograph, self-portrait

tinged sepia, she's rallying her troops, lecturing them
on how to bruise the man, drown him, make him
wear the lacy underwear, then demand he demean her.

First rule of offense: teach a man to degrade you,
you spoil his heart.

In another, she's wearing bespoke boots, stepping over the rubble
saying, *I will remember you just like this,* picking off the armor
saying, *My name is not what I said it was.*

First rule of offense: if you're never lackluster,
the enemy's never lacklusting.

Most of all, my mother wanted to live forever. No laws
or dams or mountain ranges or children are named
for her. No effigy burns, no ash is left to corrupt.
When I want to be tragic, I put on her mothworn bustier,

I cross up the brassiere, powder my face oyster-white,
roll up the tattered red stockings. I am alive then,
lifting her discarded camera. I devastate the mirror.

Four Letters from SPC Elycia Loveis Fine
(Occupied Baghdad, May 2003)

1.

It's hot. No matter the time,
no matter my state

of undress, sweat coats
my scalp, knuckles, knee-

creases, eyelids. The bathrooms
are so revolting that,

if possible, I wouldn't defecate
for the rest of my life. Even

if the pain ensured a slow death.
I put on my uniform, the gas mask,

the Kevlar helmet, two flak vests,
rubber boots, carry my rifle

down three flights, then fifty
yards out, just for the pleasure

of relieving my bladder. Fuck beds,
fuck steak; fuck movie

theaters and buttered popcorn.
I just want to flush a toilet.

2.

Iraqi air is diseased—not like Ebola-diseased,
but there are things in the air our fragile American
immune systems aren't used to.

I woke one night certain I was dying.
The medics administered two bags
of rehydration to combat the nausea.

I slept fifteen hours straight. Goetz photographed me
when I was well, on a seized palace's veranda.
Behind me, trees bloomed purple in the heat.

It isn't bad enough that Iraq makes me smelly
and angry, but it has to make me sexually
deprived too. One step at a time.

Now, I just need to work on my road rage.
Tell your mom she's a dirty whore.

3.

I sprout a new dreadlock
every five minutes and my soul

keeps trying to run away.
I'm lucky my soul isn't very smart.

Usually, I capture it before
it can cross the borders

of this fallen city. James, Baghdad
is beautiful at night.

4.

I've changed, and now my friends won't know me.
Last week I was an infantry squad member.
The mission: secure the banks.

Goetz pretended I was vital. I wasn't.
I just really wanted to go. We got lost
in the downtown marketplace throng.

My job: watch for rooftop gunmen.
It was like Mardi Gras, with fewer beads
and boobs. It's scary

how I no longer find a donkey pulling a cart
along a busy street foreign. Did you know
the Arabic for thief is *ali baba?* No lie.

While downtown, this kid driving a bus
kept licking his eleven-year-old lips at me.
I pointed my gun. I think he shit his pants.

Send more letters. Don't leave out the details
of your sex life. Please, no more tootsie rolls.
You must understand. I'm living through you.

Portrait of My Mother as Victorine Meurent

1. Street Singer

Each detail belongs to me, my easel—this is how the artist thinks.
Even the nicotine stains on her fingers,
even her delicate but practical underwear.

On every canvas, he punishes her form. In this frame,
my mother sells the undersweetness of lace against thigh,
a common street singer. *I want her, an obstacle in the afternoon*
avenues, stopping traffic in her blueblack gown. It's beginning
to rain; the passersby huddle closer.

But that doesn't stop my mother, buried in the model's
unmodest body, from singing. The artist doesn't think,
Do I always shade her with damage? Of course the men
want to entangle themselves between her thighs; of course
they want to be the one high, clear note in the song,

to plait their pain with resonance. *I never paint*
their pudgy chins, their receding hairlines. A man sidles up,
he pays her on a side street. *Have I made him cruel enough,*
will he heave her dress up to her stomach, will he touch her

thinking, Now I am her conqueror, now I am painting
the loudest part quiet in the rush of commerce,

I am disquieting her under the eaves? *Thinking,* My fingertips
will bruise her naked arms, her body will sing my hands for weeks.

Why must it always be *raining,* why is he *cruel?* Can't the artist
paint them in *love,* meaning *the timid heat between them, the man
is my father, they touch in the soundless place—*

why not *brushing a leaf off of her dress?* Why does every woman
he paints look at me with my mother's sunken eyes?
Eating too-ripe cherries, singing in the street.

The dress: will she burn it or bury it,
will she dye it red?

2. Mlle. Victorine en Costume d'Espada

Sunday morning, the arena full.
From where my mother watches
in her *traje de luces*, the thronged men
squirm, waiting for her entrance.

In her red suit, my mother is all sequined curtain-shine.
She says, *I want to die.* Looking as if she believes she could
disappear and the world would understand.
As if someone else would come to kill the bull,
as if anyone else could make it art.

You don't have the guts to pull the trigger, I've seen your mouth
closed around the barrel, you're a warrior, for Chrissakes,
pull it then, pull the goddamn—

I want to say, but all I manage is a mangled, *Be careful.*
Pointing to the pen where the dumb bull
snarls, over-decorated, pawing the earth,
He's destined to gore you.

My mother does not blink. She is the mouth
where all blood leads. She is the thirsty god
and she wants to die, and who will keep
the stained rapier, the emptied veins, the echoing in them?

I want to die, she says, holding her stomach.
Meaning, I have to die too. But now we're facing
the crowd and the men are on their feet.

And now I'm the bull, charging toward her
at full gallop, trying to make her live again.
I bellow, bring my head low against her stomach

and wait for it to happen: the blood washing over me
like a cape, the sword meeting my aorta: I'm free.
Everywhere, her name throbbing. My mother,
favorite model of Edouard Manet, the death of the charging bull.

3. *Le déjuener sur l'herbe*

Victorine refuses the baskets men bring,
they sit untouched on the starched picnic cloth,
the cheese knives glimmering at the edge of grass.

The men wear lawyer's tweed, talk of marriage.
My mother rids herself of clothing.

She is the unwanted lunch, the ant-ridden flesh,
a dream invading the picture, swimming below
the surface of the men's sight.

Underneath their talk, my mother fantasizes
into life a bather: a woman wading upstream,
dipping down her ivory haunches, water-darkening
her white dress. The current pulls and pulls at her.

My mother knows the bather belongs to her
the way spring owns its songbirds. The trees
drink her in, dissolving the bather in the watercourse.
Once they possess her, they will not give her back.

4. Olympia

The men are doomed.

They cannot take off their rumpled suits,
their grave hats, their impossible trousers,
they go on loving her—calling it love, using that word.

They keep inventing her name
with razors in the fleshy part of their forearms.
They go on, adding desolate to desperate.

Olympia reclines, her naked body rinses the eye
with an ethereal sheen. Then the maidservant appears,
her palms pink in the basket she's brought
from the garden, blooms from some hybrid bush.

The maidservant's mouth is agape: an entrance.
No one sees my mother slip her skin, draping it
over the other woman. The men go on loving her
absented body, fighting over it, flicking out their razors
and circling each other in the back of badly lit bars.

My mother will do the same for the maid. She'll go out
of the frame and fall in love with a kind man, and, knowing
she can't stay, she will undo him.

The women are sisters. They have lain together,
watching the man fumble with the belt, the buttons,
the sheepskin condom. They have been decoys,
they have suffered under the stark monopoly of light.

5. *Le Bar aux Folies-Bergère*

My mother stares at the men, her customers,
from behind the bar, the paint, the mirror.

She stares into their eyes, sees herself pinned
by their looking. Sees herself made

into an artifact, unearthed and catalogued.
She stares and says, *I am not satisfied. I am not nothing.*

The artist sees her in the bathhouses, in line at the opera,
between the lines of music, on the sidewalk

of an empty city, hesitating to cross the street,
serving drinks at every all-night café in Paris,

speechmaking in Parliament, naked
and hysterical, pointing at her open mouth—

6. *Girl on a Horse*

My mother breaks the model's pose, rising
from her seat. The sun behind her diminishes the hills.

Already her feet lift and push into shoes, her knees bend
to collect her scattered blouses. Already the horse's head
turns toward the vanishing point, far down the road

of the painting. At the canvas's blackened edge, she turns
to look back. Something waits to intercept;

two horses whose bodies have passed into the invisible
lean their graceful heads out from the end of myth.

She shakes the layers of oil from her frame, absents herself
of brushstroke, dismounts the horse, turns it free.

Her back graduates from the beautiful to the imperceptible.

She lifts one heavy leg, as if stepping from a too-cold bath.
She does not look back, she steps softly

out of the painting, out of the eye,
out of my life forever.

Aubade

A man's fingers hover over the wrong keys.

Songs have been crafted out of tonight:
the handful of imperious grackles strutting about
the trash-flanked street, your skin imitating ash
at the edge of your elbow.

My wanting grays when you part
the thin pastel curtain to join me in bed.

I miss the songs that do not save us from decay.
My percussive tongue playing
the tiny black reeds on your chin.

The piano is incessant, stumbling, dulled
through the floorboards. We take turns mocking
our need, relinquishing our bodies:

your left testicle for a right note, my left lung
for a moment's quiet. Then we imagine
replacements. *Instead of piano*, you say,
I'd rather get a whipping from my momma.
I quiet. *Instead of piano*, I say, and can't finish.

Unsure fingers search in the dark.
You stroke my hair from my forehead
and ask me why I never say I love you back.

I lie in the dark, then I do what I always do,
I move, making space for heartbreak.

Then you move with me, until our bodies touch
in the ruins where I miss aching for a god.

The End of Myth

I ask Dustin to recall his favorite memory
of our mother. He's distracted from the past,
playing a Nintendo game where what you are
is descended from a long line of monsters. The mother
is an incongruous order of unforgivable monster.

In the myths, the mother is the birth of vengeance.
I remember her flicking the end of a cigarette,
holding in the smoke, its billowing silver paths.

I knew my mother could never die. She remains
immortal, grieving the hero's bum ankle, the wasted effort
to transcend Planned Narratives.

The myths do not instruct us in forgiveness. They only say
whose wrath is wedded to whose form.

I survived my mother's suicide attempts, I lived
for years in the damage. I ate well. I quit smoking.
I loved a quiet man badly.

The heavens did not alter, the master pattern
remained untorn. The myths don't turn a man
into a hero; they take him by his sweat-stained tunic-front
and raise him into a clutch of pearled light.

My body never left the ground. I wasn't given
the kind of form you'd long for
should you among your brethren be sent to slay the Furies.

The Dumb Body

My father's limp body permits the plastic tube to bruise his scrotum
the color of rotting plum as it travels into his blocked heart,

where the blood clots his right ventricle and a camera captures every stutter
and someone's masked mouth sounds directions—

while all of this keeps over-happening in the sterile second floor
of a nearby hospital, while my father's brain hemorrhages

from the clot blasters Dr. Iftakar administered to save his diseased heart,
I am making love to my boyfriend in my father's bed.

This is the room my father could not breathe in.

I won't describe the wedding pictures nailed to the wall.
I won't remember the doctor's names. Not here, in this space

of unfurled moans. Now, where we touch we stop feeling.
The dumb body is all entrance, thigh pressing thigh, leg parted

to leg, body quickening into heat. Father, we came here
broken. Now, nothing can make us whole.

You Send Me Roses

Every window opens
out onto the red

and terrible things
of this world growing

disaffected.
My mouth is a vase.

My Father's Time

My life is three minutes slow, a stalled clock
on the dim cinderblock wall in the waiting room.
My father is doled out in increments, along with
the doctors' pronouncements: *neural complications,*
the tectonic crash of *interhemispheric hemorrhage.* My father lives

beneath these words, more still than sculpture.
A thin tube runs from his skull into a translucent bag.
I apply Blistex to his cracked lips. His chalky tongue
laps up the light coat of moisture, proof his body is gone

automatic. The few times my father told me
he loved me, I didn't say it back. I wanted to hurt him.
I sit on his bed, bring my face to his, and when I say it,
nothing returns to me except his breath.

I want to hurt my father, I know pain can lead
his way back to living. The rash around his wrists tells me
my father's body has chained him deep in his flesh.
The blood drips from a world I can't know, where nothing

is cemented and said. There the dry earth holds
the demolished as if the wreck could still be inhabited,
we could still be afflicted with time.

My father did come back.
And the body was changed. And now I'll never tell my father
because the words have changed. They died, they didn't come back—
not even crippled, not even blinking

twice for yes, once for no, three times for
I need you, please write this down.

We Exult in Your Pain

My father wears my former shirt—his chest sparkles
in basement light—and my mother displays pale thigh
where her leather miniskirt parts.

They are bathed in red neon from the sign over the door:
"We Exult in Your Pain." In the waiting room
of Dominant Divas, a jail converted into "equipped salons,"
my father takes my mother's hand, and they descend
into the dungeon below the city, into the primal cave.

When my father tells me this story,
he can't stop looking at his hands.
He can't hold a pencil, let alone a whip.

He sits in his wheelchair. He can't
stop looking at his hands.
All his stories happen before

my mother left him, when he didn't sleep
in a hospital bed in an apartment
that disability pays for. He tells me

he chose the stock whip.
He says my mother screamed.

The Enemy

Dustin couldn't stand to be alone, we were twins.
Or not twins. But people mistook us because the Fates
are lazy, full of the whimsy that drives an experimental nature—
they marked one like the other.

As when I walked away to use the bathroom, my brother fixed
to my shirttail until I promised he could come too, though I made him
stand in the corner of the bathtub, the shower curtain drawn.

And now the curtain slides back, you see the scene
is changed. We are in a kitchen on a Friday night,
slicing cucumbers for a salad. We're older, our bodies
have grown harder, we cut without provocation.

Now no one mistakes us. I'd know my brother in any room
by the sadness he takes pains to bury,
by the way he holds a knife.

You can't make something as breakable as a heart
without a prototype, a twin.

You can't leave it hidden in the earth—
it calls and calls for the other.

But because the Fates enjoy verisimilitude as much
as violence, the other heart is also buried, only half as deep.

My brother is so beautiful with the knives.
He can't help making everything he holds a weapon.
He sent flowers, and still the man he loved would not return.

I know you think the twin is only a figure of speech,
that I'm telling you this while avoiding your eyes.
But it's real, it's a question, it marked us in time:

How could my father not have known
my mother did not love him?

When the man said "I love you," Dustin dug himself out,
he said it back. But he hadn't healed. He couldn't say it
without meaning something else. And what he meant was,
Now you're the enemy.

And now the shower curtain is yours, you're listening to me
and you think I'm telling you the truth. I've said the intimate things.
I've gripped you. I will hurt you now,
pull you down here in the hollow the rain made in the dirt.

Look at us, skin against skin, afraid.

Look at me, my cheek on your chest,
waiting for you to sleep. I'm listening to your heart,
the sad liar in you now, the twin arteries
cutting the body its two paths. I'm listening in your blood.

Naming the End

I love you either begins the lecture on ancient torture
or reveals the way back to Eve, who spends her last night
naming the flora, stenciling their anatomies
on her husband's somnolent skin. The husband is a god.

At daybreak, they abandon the garden. He carries into the world
the only diagram we'll ever have for devotion. In the dark
interrupted by sirens, I plant words you'll never know
you carry on your back. At dawn, you open your eyes

to the light in which you'll leave me. You rinse that other world
of steam and whisper from your skin. Soon, you're filling
your dented black car with all your clothes, all your records
and books and love. When you leave, your skin repeats: *I love you.*

Gods never sleep and terrible fates await us.
You get to choose. Once.

Love the Shattered Thing

My boyfriend leaves me. I grieve days, a week
—the way my father did, when my mother left.

I sleep on the floor. I turn on all the lights.
In the morning, I make too much coffee.

The emptiness enters me again. But then
he's back. I am so glad to have him enter

my body again, I do not punish him.
I forgive him so he does not have to ask.

Then he's gone. Then he's back. I keep letting him go,
letting him return. If I learn to love the shattered thing

inside him, maybe he won't leave.
If I learn the shattered thing inside him

is me, my demand to have him make me
something broken, something whole,

I wouldn't take him back. I wouldn't let us become
the shards of my parents' cliché: the more one leaves,

the more love roots in the one who stays.
The door my boyfriend enters back to me

is the door my parents made. Rusted gate
won't shut no matter how much you force it.

It lets in the flies, the rot, every trust. One day,
I won't be able to close. I won't open. Numb man

in his shoddy wheelchair, unable to climb
out of the rising water, out of the porcelain tub

holding him in stasis—my mother there to dry him,
to wipe his mouth, his ass.

Portrait of My Lover Singing in Traffic

Man rushing onto Sunrise Boulevard, singing Disorder
in the Flesh: first threadbare notes, then his trousers

stunning the air—man singing the Jackknifed Torso,
Stabbed Back songs, man jerking between rows of cars,

people locking their doors, their faces ashen
when at last his shirt comes off. Wind carrying the ripped bar

of fabric to the sidewalk where I catch him, fitting fingers
to places his skin had been. Man rushing into traffic

losing his shoes, their holes like something singed.
Then his underwear. Then he's naked, I Ain't Got No Body.

Everyone watching, moving their lips, the train guards
lowering the song of the mechanical flashing arm,

stopping all of us. The muscle of him unstoppable,
uncontrollable song. Sirens reddening air,

a mouth opening back the counterweight song, I Been Rent
by Tougher Men, which becomes so quickly the Gravelmouth,

the Spreadleg, the Ribkicked song, which gives way behind glass
in the police cruiser to the I've Been Your Bulletproof

Piece of Ass, Now Take Me to Where I'll Die
in Shadow song. Inside my shattershot skin I sing

the broken ballads my mother taught me: My Body Severed
in Fogsway, the Derailed Train Is My Shepherd,

I Shall Not Want, her voice audible even under all that
copmuscle and metal, singing the Song of Stained

and Never More Beautiful Than Criminal, and the man
is my mother, I'm filled with want. The lyrics are rushing

unbidden out of me, joining the shirtless choir in the street,
all hands locking, webbed behind the head, face between the legs

kicked apart, singing Don't Grieve So Open,
in motherless tones, right on through from the beginning.

"Portrait of My Mother as the Republic of Texas" (p. 5): The Republic of Texas, an actual organization still thriving in Cuero, Texas, refuses to acknowledge their state's 1865 admission into the Union. Fiercely independent and yet strangely conservative, these rebels fly in the face of convention even while asserting the validity of their own politically left traditions. The poem is for Tamara Fish.

"Portrait of My Mother as Rosemary Woodhouse" (p. 9) owes a debt to *Rosemary's Baby* (Roman Polanski, 1968). All quotes appear in the film.

"A Fact Which Occurred in America" (p. 14): George Dawe's full title is *A Negro Overpowering a Buffalo—A Fact Which Occurred in America, 1809.* In Dawe's depiction, which he based on a reportedly true story, we see a black man pinning a buffalo to the ground, his shoulders and head hunched over the animal. We see only the buffalo's face: he turns one red, terrified eye up toward his violator. Something about the painting—including the correspondence it makes between the darkness of the man's skin and the buffalo's fur—highlights for me the untenable situation for either of the characters. The poem is for Catherine Barnett.

"Portrait of My Mother as Self-Inflicting Philomena" (p. 17) is for Beth Ferda, Caitlin Franklin, and Sam Vuchenich.

"Portrait of My Lover as 'Man in a Polyester Suit (1980)'" (p. 41): Robert Mapplethorpe's famous photograph, "Man in a Polyester Suit (1980)," shows an African American man in a slightly rumpled three-piece suit. The image is cropped from the chest to just above the knees, and the undone zipper shows a large, semi-erect, uncircumcised penis.

"Portrait of My Mother as Virginia Lillian Mountweazel" (p. 43): Mountweazel (1942–1973) is a fictitious character inserted into the 1975 *New Columbia Encyclopedia* in order to thwart copycats. Born in Bangs, Ohio, her entry also indicates she was a U.S. fountain designer and photographer. Mountweazel died in an explosion while on assignment for *Combustibles* magazine.

"Portrait of My Mother as Victorine Meurent" (p. 49): Victorine Meurent (1844–1927) sat for eight of Manet's paintings, including *Olympia* (1863), *déjuener sur l'herbe* (1863), *Mlle. Victorine en Costume d'Espada* (1862), *Street Singer* (1862, the first painting for which she sat), and *The Railway* (1873, the last). Meurent, herself an artist, showed at three Paris Salons, though little of her work survives. Her identity has been obscured, even replaced, by the images she modeled.